Commissioned by the Carnegie Hall Corporation

First performed March 2, 2000 by Kirill Gerstein
at the world premiere of the Carnegie Hall Millennium Piano Book,
Weill Recital Hall, New York City

RECORDINGS

Ursula Oppens: Carnegie Hall Millennium Piano Book
Boosey & Hawkes, Inc., ISMN 051-24617-5 (CD enclosed)

Charles Rosen: Bridge Records 9128

Winston Choi: l'empreinte digitale ED13164

Duration: 8 minutes

NOTE BY THE COMPOSER

These *Two Diversions* for piano deal with a growing contrast between simultaneous musical ideas. The first *Diversion* presents a line of paired notes, musical intervals, that maintain a single speed throughout, while the other very changeable material uses many different speeds and characters. The second *Diversion* contrasts two musical lines one of which, on the whole, grows slower and slower while the other grows faster and faster. With these musical ideas about diverging materials, I hope I have written diverting music.

—Elliott Carter

ANMERKUNG DES KOMPONISTEN

In diesen beiden Divertimenti für Klavier wird der wachsende Kontrast zwischen simultanen musikalischen Ideen behandelt. So gibt es im ersten Divertimento eine Linie mit Notenpaaren in musikalischen Intervallen, die ein gleichbleibendes Tempo durchhalten, während das übrige Material viele verschiedene Tempi und Charaktere vorstellt. Im zweiten Divertimento werden zwei musikalische Linien einander gegenübergestellt, von denen die eine immer langsamer und die andere immer schneller wird. Durch diese musikalischen Ideen mit verschiedenen Materialien ist es mir hoffentlich gelungen, unterhaltsame Musik zu schreiben.

—Elliott Carter

NOTE DU COMPOSITEUR

Ces *Two Diversions* pour piano portent sur un contraste croissant entre des idées musicales simultanées. La première *Diversion* présente une ligne de notes couplées, des intervalles musicaux, qui restent au même tempo d'un bout à l'autre, pendant que les autres éléments très changeants ont de nombreux tempos et caractères différents. La seconde *Diversion* fait contraster deux lignes musicales dont l'une devient dans l'ensemble de plus en plus lente, tandis que l'autre devient de plus en plus rapide. Au moyen de ces idées musicales sur des éléments divergents, j'espère avoir écrit de la musique divertissante.

—Elliott Carter

ELLIOTT CARTER

TWO DIVERSIONS

for solo piano

HENDON MUSIC

BOOSEY & HAWKES

DISTRIBUTED BY

Hal•Leonard®

ELLIOTT CARTER

TWO DIVERSIONS

for solo piano

www.boosey.com
www.halleonard.com

HENDON MUSIC

7777 W. BLUEMOUND RD. P.O. BOX 13819 MILWAUKEE, WI 53213

for Ursula Oppens

TWO DIVERSIONS
I

Elliott Carter
(1999)

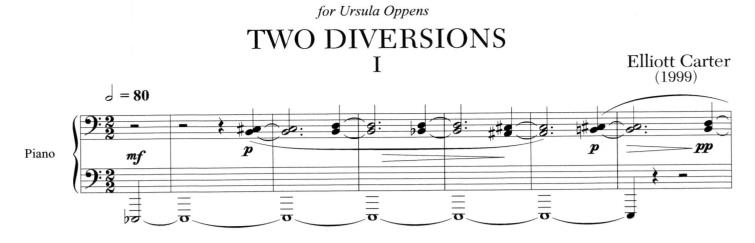

M-051-24624-3

Printed in U.S.A.

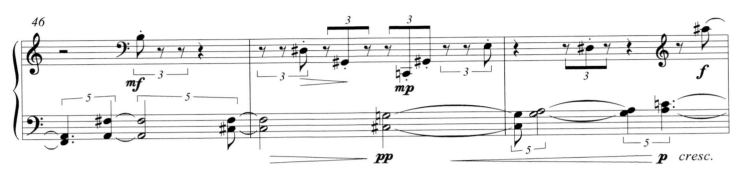

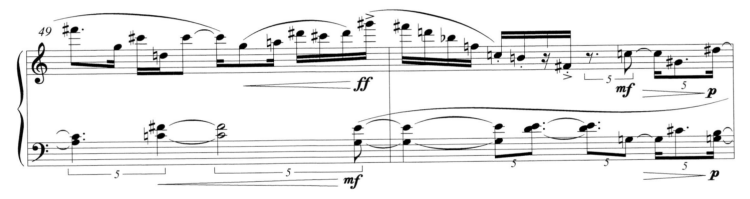

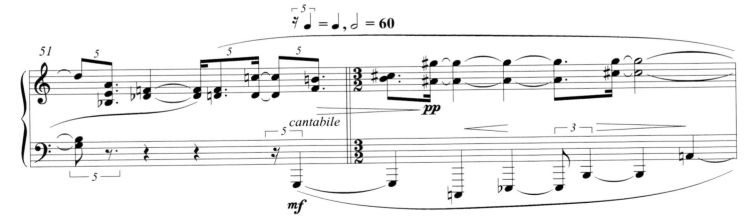

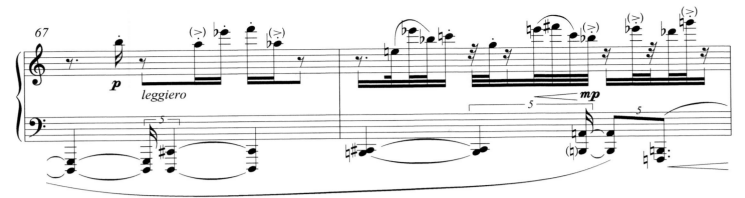

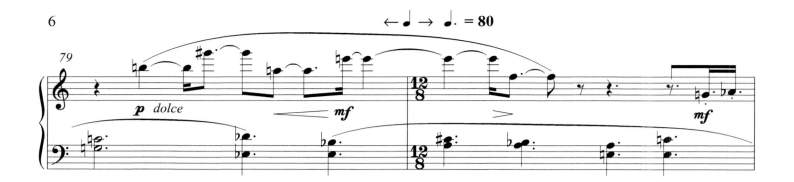

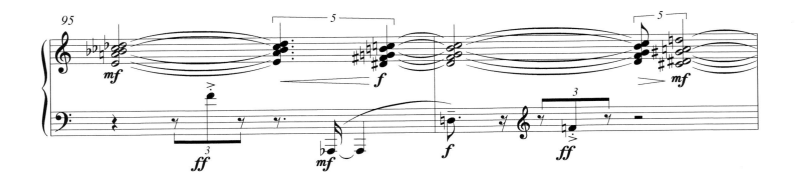

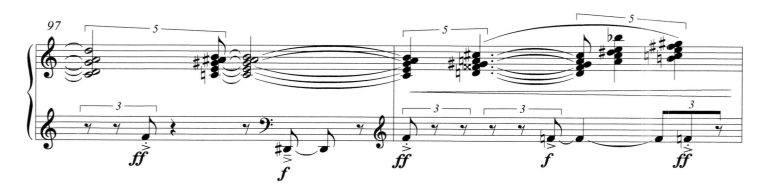

II

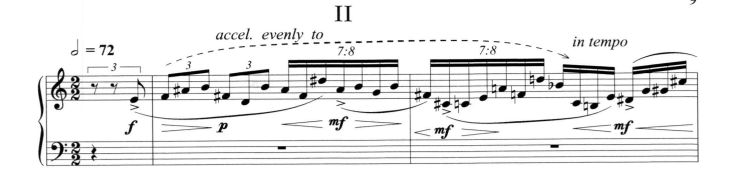

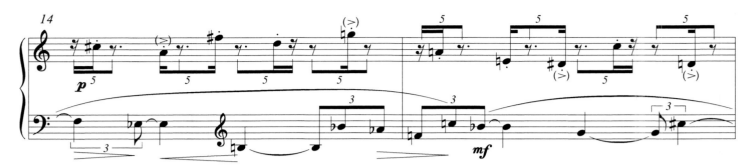

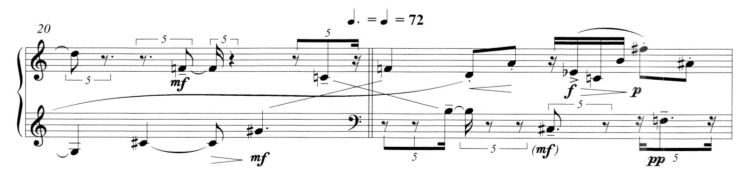

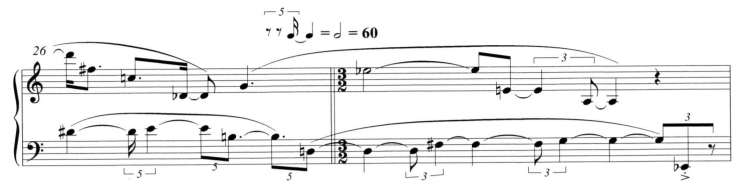

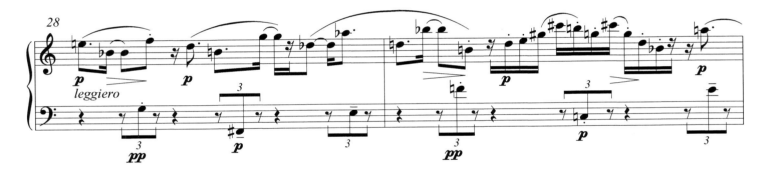

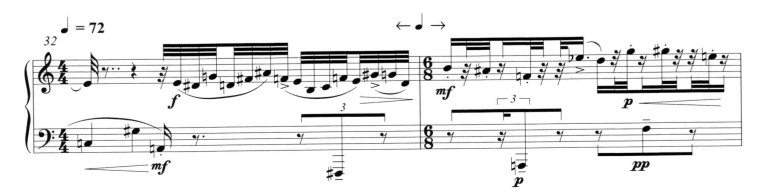

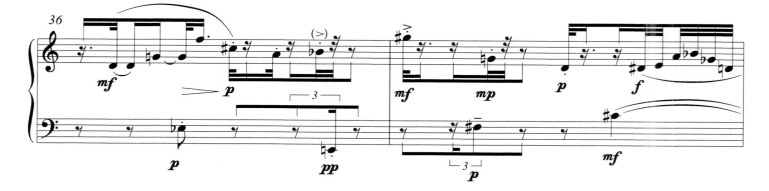

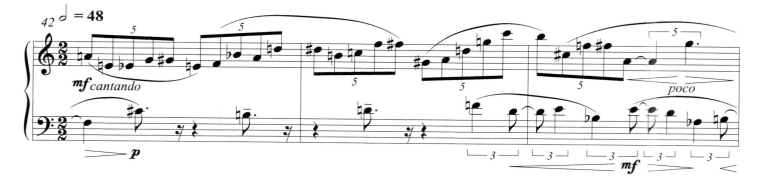

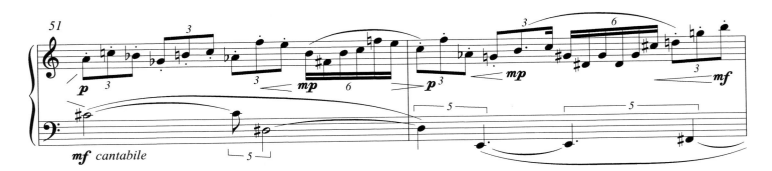

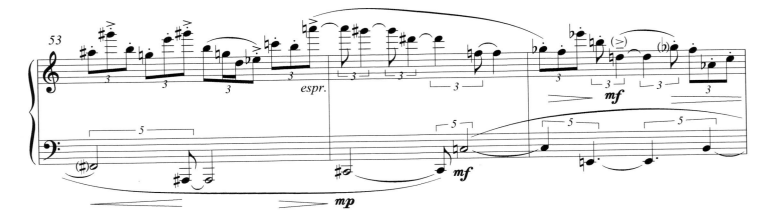

14

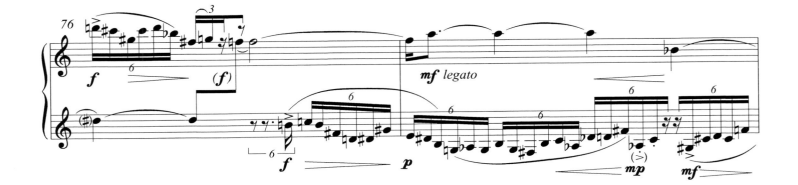

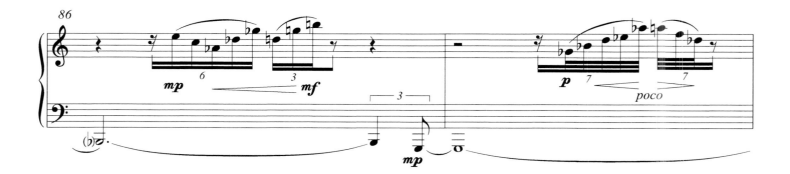

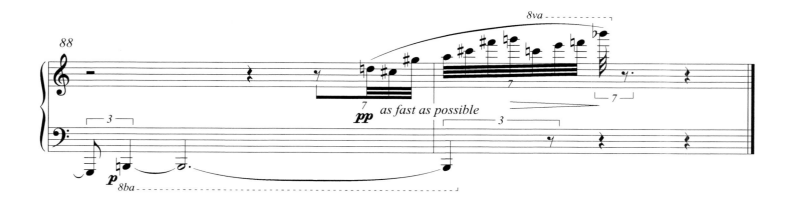

CHAMBER MUSIC OF
ELLIOTT CARTER

TRIPLE DUO (1983)   20'
for flute (doubling piccolo), clarinet (doubling E♭ and bass clarinets), percussion, piano, violin, and cello

CHANGES (1983)   7'
for guitar

CANON FOR 4 (1984)   4'
"Homage to William"
for flute, bass clarinet, violin and cello

RICONOSCENZA PER GOFFREDO
   PETRASSI (1984)   4'
for solo violin

ESPRIT RUDE / ESPRIT DOUX (1984)   4'
pour Pierre Boulez
for flute and B♭ clarinet

STRING QUARTET NO. 4 (1986)   24'

ENCHANTED PRELUDES (1988)   6'
for flute and cello

BIRTHDAY FLOURISH (1988)   1'
for five trumpets or brass quintet

CON LEGGEREZZA PENSOSA (1990)   5'
Omaggio a Italo Calvino
for B♭ clarinet, violin, and cello

SCRIVO IN VENTO (1991)   5'
for solo flute

QUINTET (1991)   20'
for piano and winds

TRILOGY (1992)   17'
   Bariolage *for solo harp*   7'
   Inner Song *for solo oboe*   5'
   Immer Neu *for oboe and harp*   5'

GRA (1993)   4'
for solo B♭ clarinet

GRA (1993)   4'
transcribed for trombone by Benny Sluchin

TWO FIGMENTS
for solo cello
   No. 1 (1994)   5'
   No. 2 – Remembering Mr. Ives (2001)   3'

TWO FRAGMENTS
for string quartet
   No. 1 – in memoriam David Huntley (1994)   4'
   No. 2 (1999)   3'

ESPRIT RUDE / ESPRIT DOUX II (1994)   5'
for flute, clarinet and marimba

OF CHALLENGE AND OF LOVE (1995)   25'
five poems of John Hollander
for soprano and piano

STRING QUARTET NO. 5 (1995)   20'

A 6 LETTER LETTER (1996)   3'
for solo English horn

QUINTET (1997)   10'
for piano and string quartet

LUIMEN (1997)   12'
for trumpet, trombone, mandolin, guitar, harp, and vibraphone

SHARD (1997)   3'
for solo guitar

TEMPO E TEMPI (1998)   15'
for soprano, violin, English horn, and bass clarinet

FRAGMENT NO. 2 (1999)   3'
for string quartet

TWO DIVERSIONS (1999)   8'
for solo piano

RETROUVAILLES (2000)   3'
for solo piano

4 LAUDS (1984-2000)   11'
for solo violin
   Statement – Remembering Aaron (1999)   3'
   Riconoscenza per Goffredo Petrassi (1984)   4'
   Rhapsodic Musings (2000)   2'
   Fantasy – Remembering Roger (1999)   3'

OBOE QUARTET (2001)   17'
for oboe, violin, viola, and cello

HIYOKU (2001)   4'
for two clarinets

STEEP STEPS (2001)   3'
for bass clarinet

AU QUAI (2002)   3'
for bassoon and viola

RETRACING (2002)   3'
for solo bassoon

CALL (2003)   1'
for two trumpets and horn

INTERMITTENCES (2005)   6'
for solo piano

HENDON MUSIC

BOOSEY & HAWKES

U.S. $10.95

HL48019130

DISTRIBUTED BY
HAL•LEONARD® CORPORATION
7777 W. BLUEMOUND RD. P.O. BOX 13819 MILWAUKEE, WI 53213

ISBN-13: 978-1-4234-1038-6
Distributed By
HAL LEONARD
48019130   9 781423 410386

ISMN M-051-24624-3